TOOLS FOR CAREGIVERS

- **F&P LEVEL:** D
- **WORD COUNT:** 45

- **CURRICULUM CONNECTIONS:** animals, habitats, nature

Skills to Teach

- **HIGH-FREQUENCY WORDS:** a, and, are, eat, have, I, in, it, my, one, see, they, up
- **CONTENT WORDS:** baby, backyard, called, ears, fast, fluffy, grass, grow, help, kits, legs, long, nest, rabbits, run, short, tails, whiskers
- **PUNCTUATION:** exclamation points, periods
- **WORD STUDY:** long a, spelled ai (tails); long e, spelled ea (ears, eat); long e, spelled ee (see); long e, spelled y (baby, fluffy); long o, spelled ow (grow); compound word (backyard)
- **TEXT TYPE:** information report

Before Reading Activities

- Read the title and give a simple statement of the main idea.
- Have students "walk" though the book and talk about what they see in the pictures.
- Introduce new vocabulary by having students predict the first letter and locate the word in the text.
- Discuss any unfamiliar concepts that are in the text.

After Reading Activities

Ask readers if they have ever seen a rabbit. Where was it? What color was it? Have readers draw a picture to show where the rabbit was and what it was doing. Have each reader show his or her picture and explain what it shows. If readers haven't seen a rabbit, have them draw one based off of the photographs in the book.

Tadpole Books are published by Jump!, 5357 Penn Avenue South, Minneapolis, MN 55419, www.jumplibrary.com

Copyright ©2020 Jump. International copyright reserved in all countries. No part of this book may be reproduced in any form without written permission from the publisher.

Editor: Jenna Trnka   **Designer:** Michelle Sonnek

Photo Credits: Tsekhmister/Shutterstock, cover; Voren1/iStock, 1; Landshark1/Shutterstock, 2tr, 3; Eric Isselee/Shutterstock, 2tl, 2bl, 2br, 4–5; frans lemmens/Alamy, 6–7; Leena Robinson/Shutterstock, 8–9; paigemcfadden/iStock, 2mr, 10–11; Oleksandr Lytvynenko/Shutterstock, 2ml, 12–13; Simeon 69/Shutterstock, 14–15; Geza Farkas/Shutterstock, 16.

Library of Congress Cataloging-in-Publication Data
Names: Nilsen, Genevieve, author.
Title: Rabbits / by Genevieve Nilsen.
Description: Tadpole edition. | Minneapolis, MN: Jump!, Inc., (2020) | Series: Backyard animals | Audience: Age 3–6. | Includes index.
Identifiers: LCCN 2019016665 (print) | LCCN 2019018520 (ebook) | ISBN 9781645271048 (ebook) | ISBN 9781645271024 (hardcover: alk. paper) | ISBN 9781645271031 (paperback)
Subjects: LCSH: Rabbits—Juvenile literature.
Classification: LCC QL737.L32 (ebook) | LCC QL737.L32 N55 2020 (print) | DDC 599.32—dc23
LC record available at https://lccn.loc.gov/2019016665

RABBITS

by Genevieve Nilsen

TABLE OF CONTENTS

tadpole
books

WORDS TO KNOW

ears

fluffy

kits

nest

tails

whiskers

RABBITS

Rabbits are fluffy.

tail

They have short tails.

ears

whiskers

They have long ears and whiskers.

Rabbits run fast!

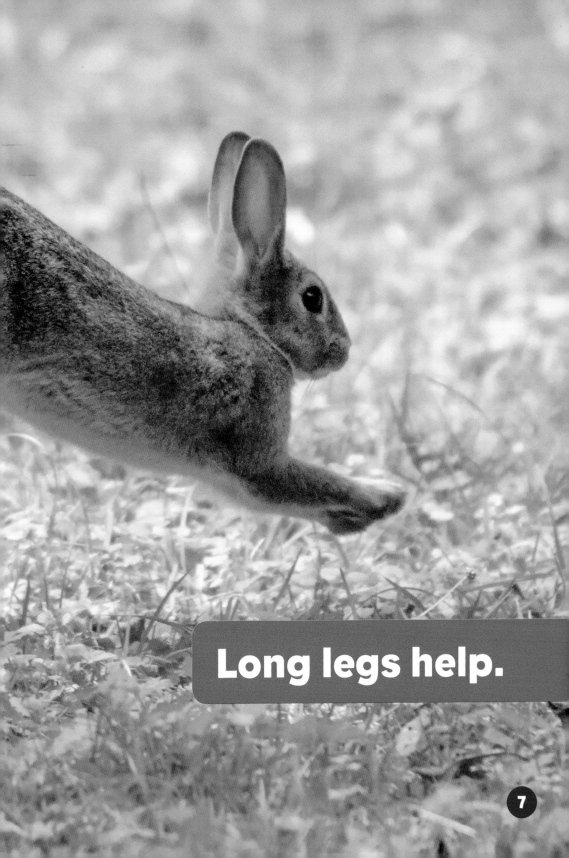

Long legs help.

They eat grass.

nest

I see a nest!

Baby rabbits are in it!

kit

They are called kits.

They grow up.